INTRODUCTION

CW00341367

This is our nineteenth book, and complied after many request;
We have included Postcards from our collection and from our
to Mrs Noel Harris of Filton, with pictures and information or
John who lent us many pictures from his and the Filton Cam
we have included in this book. We enjoyed talking to him and his m....
Aircraft Industry. We are sorry he did not live to see this book in print.

ACKNOWLEDGEMENTS

Our Sincere Thanks to Mrs Noel Harris for the use of pictures No 22. 33.
Our Sincere Thanks to the late Mr Russell John for the use of pictures No 25. 26. 38. 46. 47. 70. 71. 72.
Our Sincere Thanks to Mr Michael Lambert for the use of pictures No 60. 62. 63. 66.
Our Sincere Thanks to Mr Andrew Palmer for the use of pictures No 3. 18. 20. 21. 58.
Our Sincere Thanks to Mr Alan (Tom) Sawyer for the use of pictures No 9. 15. 24. 36. 37. 44.

BIBLIOGRAPHY

Filton Gloucestershire W. L. Harris, Filton Footsteps Noel Harris, Filton and the Flying Machine complied by Malcolm Hall, Filton to Severn Beach in old Photographs Complied by John Hudson, Field guide Railways of the Western Region by Geoffrey Body.

FRONT COVER PICTURE No 17
BACK COVER TOP PICTURE No 73
BACK COVER BOTTOM PICTURE No 84

For further details of all our Publications and for photographs from this book, or any other book visit us on our web site www.bygonebristol.co.uk.

FILTON

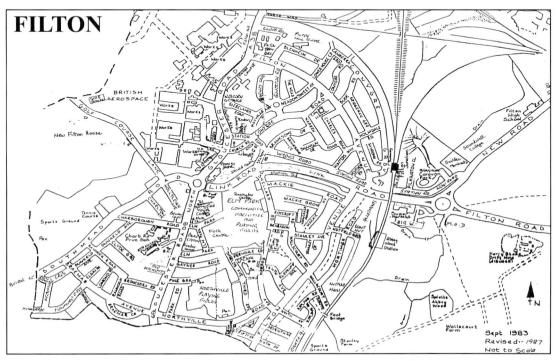

Sept 1983
Revised 1987
Not to Scale

FILTON

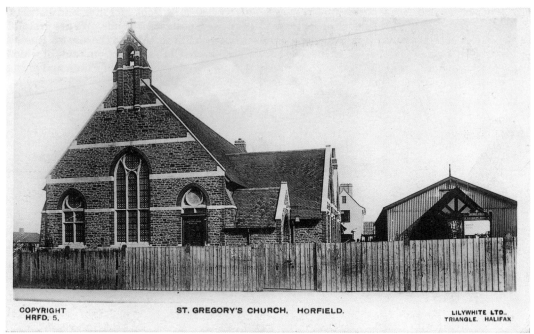

1. St Gregory the Great in Filton Road, situated beyond Montreal Avenue, on the right hand side. The church dating from 1911.

2. Filton Road council houses built in the 1930's , with the grounds of Monks Park School on the left hand side of the road.

BRAEMAR AVENUE, HORFIELD.

COPYRIGHT HRFD. 4.

LILYWHITE LTD. TRIANGLE HALIFAX

3. Braemar Avenue Horfield, but the road comes within the Filton Boundary. This road is on the corner of Filton Road, on the opposite corner the site of old Cabot Cinema.

COPYRIGHT HRFD. 7

NORTHVILLE ROAD, HORFIELD.

LILYWHITE LTD., TRIANGLE, HALIFAX.

4. Northville Road runs parallel with Braemar Avenue, off Filton Road. The houses built in the 1930s. This road is also within the Filton boundary.

5. Eden Grove the houses built in the pre war period. The road extends from Filton Road, and crosses Filton Avenue. It joins Wordsworth Avenue and Eighth Avenue. The postcard written and posted in 1943 to Redruth in Cornwall.

6. Filton Avenue, the postcard written in 1938 and sent to Halburton in Devon. Houses and shops newly built, the shops on the right, Clatcote Farm Dairy and the shop next door owned by J F Hopkins.

A GEORGES HOUSE. 'THE FELLOWSHIP INN.'

7. The Fellowship Inn, situated on the corner of Toronto Road, was built in 1929. The sign "The Fellowship", is a ship in full sail. The sign being an exact reproduction of the ill fated ship the "Herzogin Cecile".

8. Filton Avenue a view further along from picture No. 7 in the 1950s. The distinctive pillars of the "Bulldog" public house built around 1938. It was named after an Aircraft built at Filton of that name.

COPYRIGHT
HRFD 12   ST. THERESA'S R.C.   CHURCH, FILTON.   LILYWHITE LTD
                                                                                    TRIANGLE

9. St Teresa's Roman Catholic Church opened in October 1927 by Canon Williams Lee. It was considered a temporary church, until enough money could be raised to build a more permanent church. This first church was built on a site known as the "Wicketts".

10. This postcard is a drawing of the proposed new church of St Teresa's. In 1945 Dennis Lucy, the appointed parish priest worked to raise money to erect a permanent church from this design. A house was purchased in 1956 and pulled down to make way for the new church, which was opened by the Bishop of Clifton in 1960. The original church is now the church hall, used for social functions and meetings.

11. The Cabot Cinema in Gloucester Road North, was opened in October 1935, after many years and showing a great variety of films it closed in 1961, after service as a supermarket, it was pulled down and replaced by shops, with accommodation above for students of the University of the West of England.

12. Gloucester Road North looking in the direction of Filton Village c 1910. The large house on the corner of Bronksea Road in use today as a hotel.

13. Filton Road, today part of Gloucester Road North, looking back towards the Cabot Cinema, which was built in 1935. These large houses built on land owned by George Elms, in the early 1900s. One house is still called "The Elms".

14. The Wesleylan Chapel built on Gloucester Road North, at the junction with Southmead Road. The ground acquired in 1916 from the land known as Townsend, and owned by Church Farm. The chapel opened in 1925, and in later years used as Filton Library.

15. An early view of Filton at the top of Filton Hill c 1905. With the post office on the left and opposite on the corner of the Old Bristol Bank.

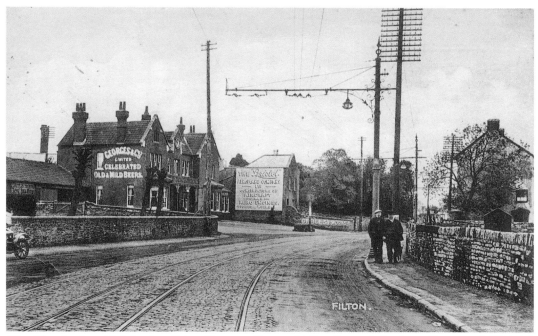

16. The Anchor Hotel advertising Georges Beer. At the far end the hoardings read "Bristol Aeroplane Company Ltd", constructors of aircraft and aero engines. The Anchor Hotel one of the earliest Inns in Filton has been pulled down and replaced by a new inn called "The Mill House".

17. A closer view of the Anchor Hotel, with its distinctive pointed roof and bay windows, a further wing was added in later years. c1916.

18. Filton Village capturing the period during the 1914-18 war.

19. Filton Village looking in the opposite direction to picture No 18. Many advertising hoardings on view, including one for "OXO", and another "Why pay rent" inviting buyers to buy their own homes, suggested prices £400-800.

20. Filton Village during 1914-18. An advertisement for furniture and carpets on the wall of the building next to the post office.

21. Filton Tram Terminus, with the chimney of Shields Laundry prominent in the distance.

22. These cottages called "The Rank", situated opposite the Bristol Aeroplane Block built in the mid 1930s. The cottages built in the mid 1800s were very small but many large families lived in them, when working on the Bristol South Wales railway extension, the line opened in 1863.

23. Samuel Shield was the founder of Filton Laundry the premises opposite the Anchor Hotel. This view in 1906 when all the deliveries were made by horse and cart. The house adjoining the laundry was Samuel Shield's home. It was later purchased by Lloyds Bank in 1954, and was demolished in 2000.

24. A early delivery van of Filton Laundry c 1916. On the side of their an advertising Dyeing, cleaning and carpet beating. The telephone number being No 3 Filton.

FILTON LAUNDRY (SAMUEL SHIELD LTD.)

25. Aerial view of Filton Laundry, showing the extensive area of the Laundry.

26. Samuel Shield's Laundry was established in 1869, on this site in Filton, and the business was carried on by his son also named Samuel, and his grandson. This view in the 1920's shows the extensive fleet of lorries owned by the laundry. The laundry closed in 1951.

27. The head office of Bristol Aeroplane Co Ltd, built c 1936. The top centre shows a model of an aircraft carved in stone, and below a carving of Pegusus, the name of the engine developed by the company.

28. A queue of cars as aircraft workers make their way home at the end of there shift, many cyclists and workers on foot. This view in the 1930s.

29. Tram No 29, at the tram terminus by Filton Church. c 1938. The hut behind removed for Church extensions, which were finished and dedicated in March 1961.

30. Tram No 54 opposite "The Rank", c 1928.

31. Filton Church c 1905. Showing the extensive grounds shortly after Cotthay had been added to the grounds. The Church bordered on one side by Station Road, and on the other side Church Road.

32. Filton Church in the 1950s. Taken from the main road before the extensions were completed in 1961.

33. The dedication of the Filton War Memorial in 1920, to commemorate those Filton men who gave there lives in the 1914-18 War. Postcard published by F Bustin of Bristol.

PARISH CHURCH, FILTON.

34. The entrance to Filton Church in Church Road, showing the unusual archway, with lamp above, and an ornate iron gate.

35. Looking down Station Road from the main road, the A 38. The wall of the church grounds on the right, and the cottage in the distance called the "Withies".

36. An early view of Station Road c 1910. The wall of the church and smoke coming from the chimney of the "Withies" cottage. Near to the left the entrance of Wades Farm.

37. Station Road a rural view, with three small boys with their home made barrow. c1912.

38. The First Filton National School built in 1850, on the corner of Station Road. The school closed in 1927 when the Charborough Road Junior School opened.

39. The top of Filton Hill, with evidence of horse drawn transport on the road!

40. Bristol Old Bank, ladies with their Trays Collecting for Alexandra Rose Day in 1916. The postcard message refers to an aircraft just visible above the telegraph pole.

41. The junction of Gloucester Road North with Southmead Road 1950. The Memorial Hall, just in view on the right, was removed to make a large roundabout joining A4174 Ring Road. The Church with it's original Tower.

42. Filton in the 1950s. The "Rank", replaced by shops, and a double decker bus replacing the Trams.

FILTON

43. The new position of Filton Road Post Office on the corner of Gloucester Road North. Removed for road improvements.

44. A mixed goods train passing through Filton Junction in the 1950's, with the signal down for a clear line.

45. This view shows the cottages at the junction of Church Road. Photograph by Garratt of Bristol.

46. Wades Road in the 1920s-30s when the road ended in fields. The Wade Family was connected with Filton for at least three centuries, Wades Road starts from Station Road, behind the flats and runs parallel with the link road until it joins Station Road again, at the corner of Hunters Way.

47. Filton Central Garage on the left at the top of Filton Hill.

48. Filton Hill c 1910. Fairlawn House on the left and further down the hill Rodney Hill Farm. The large fir tree next to the telegraph pole still survives today.

49. Filton Hill described as near Bristol c 1905. The postman with his delivery bag standing in the middle of the road.

50. The Naish Family Group taken in the front garden of Fairlawn House. The postcard written by Mr E Naish in 1906. Note the parrot included in the Family group!

51. Filton Rectory situated in the Fields adjoining Filton Hill.

52. Looking up Filton Hill c 1918. A rural view, but the bend in the road recognisable today, with the Rectory on the left.

53. Filton Hill and Rodney Hill Farm.

54. Another view from the bottom of Filton Hill. The postcard written on August 11th 1923.

THE AERODROME, FILTON.

COPYRIGHT
HRFD. 11.

LILYWHITE LTD.
TRIANGLE. HALIFAX

55. This view shows the early development of the Aircraft Buildings c 1931.

Filton Hill 1365.

56. Soldiers walking up the hill 1914-18, the fields beyond undeveloped yet. The telegraph poles, formed part of the main trunk line to Gloucester.

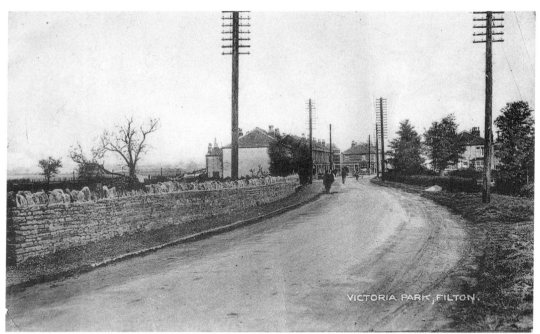

57. Victoria Park named after Queen Victoria. The postcard written and posted from Filton in 1926. The footpath from Mr Naishes house were proposed in 1909. Funds were eventually raised by the council and residents, and the pavement finished in 1912.

58. Victoria Park built in 1898. This view in 1916 in the direction of Patchway. Some of the houses destroyed in air raids during the war, the others for road widening and extension to the the factory, only the house in the centre survives as a cafe.

59. The Saw Mill Tug of War Team, practising in a field in Filton. Photograph by F Bustin of Bristol.

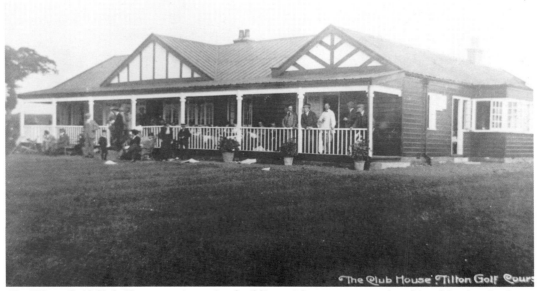

60. Filton Golf Club House, an imposing building with a strong membership, this view in the 1930s. The present Golf Club house situated at the end of Golf Course Lane, off Southmead Road.

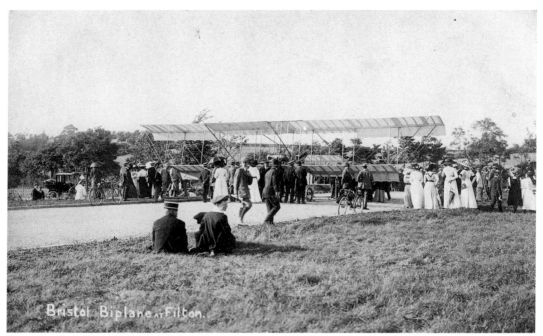

61. The British and Colonial Aeroplane Company at Filton, developed Biplanes in conjunction with Societe Francaise Zodic of Paris. The association with the French ended, after a few years the Boxkite was developed at Bristol. This view of the plane at Filton c 1910 attracting many onlookers.

62. The caption reads "What did you see at Filton? Crowds have gathered to see the "Boxkite" Biplane the first Bristol only design, which was developed by the British and Colonial Aeroplane Company, founded by Sir George White.

63. In the early years of development of the aviation industry. Britain was jointly involved with the French. The Frenchman Maurice Tetard, with his co pilot C. W. Briginshaw, made several successful flights in the Boxkite, taking off from Durdham Downs, in 1910.

THE BRISTOL "BULLDOG."

64. The "Bulldog" a single seater Fighter, built entirely from metal and fitted with a Bristol "Juniper" series V 11 Engine, it became the RAFs principal front line fighter in the early 1930s.

65. The Brabazon Hanger built in 1948-49 to house the new large passenger aeroplane of that name being built at the Filton works.

66. Filton Golf Club players on the 11th Green. The Golf Club was established in 1909, Samuel Shield of Filton Laundry, was one the founder members. Competitions were held and the trophy presented by Ernest Shield, Samuel's son.

67. Bristol Aeroplane Company new canteen block adjoining the A38 in the 1930s.

68. Bristol Flying School built on the eastern side of Gloucester Road. These schools designed to train weekend pilots, in what was then the RAF reserves.

S.20483.　　　　BRABAZON MARK I.　WING SPAN 230 FEET.　LENGTH 177 FEET.　　　Photo:-
Bristol Aeroplane Co.

69. The Brabazon Hanger was designed as a passenger aircraft to seat approximately one hundred passengers, and fly non stop to America. It was never a great success. The prototype Mark 1 flew for the first time in September 1949. Captained by the chief test pilot Bill Pegg.

70. The Brabazon hanger designed partly by Eric Ross, chief architect, c1946. The building remarkable as it lead the way of design for such a large building.

71. The Britannia first flew in 1952, and entered service in 1957. The aeroplane was a great success, about eighty were built. The first airline to operate the plane were B A O C, followed by many airlines around the world.

72. Concorde nearing completion in the Filton workshops. The most successful super-sonic plane yet built in conjunction with France in Tolouse, but first developed at Filton. The main route being the Trans Atlantic to New York.

73. Patchway on the main A 38 north from Filton, this view c 1906. The Gospel Hall on the right, large trees line the road.

74. The road bridge over the Bristol-South Wales railway line c 1906, showing the two lines at different gradients. On the right the row of cottages by the present day roundabout adjoining the railway line.

75. The first Bus service from Filton to Thornbury crossing the railway bridge at Patchway in 1906.

76. The G W R Train "Earl of Edgecombe", approaching Patchway Station in 1958. The train the Express from London Paddington to Swansea.

77. The Railway Hotel adjoining the Bristol-South Wales line on the main A 38 north. A Georges Inn serving not only wines and spirits but teas c 1906.

78. The extensive garden at the back of the Railway Hotel, summer houses around the edge of the garden. Popular with walkers and cyclists with overnight accommodation available c 1906.

BIRKHILL
CLAY
MINE

Underground experience!

FOR AN UNFORGETTABLE DAY OUT!

Discover the secrets of Fireclay deep in the underground tunnels at the heart of the mine. See 300-million-year-old fossils, and learn how miners worked the clay.

Clay Mine Opening Times:

Weekends: From 14th April - 14th. October
Saturdays and Sundays 12.30 -4.00

Daily: From 16th July - 31st. August
Mondays - Saturdays 11.30 - 4.00
Sundays 12.30 - 4.00

We welcome pre-booked parties outwith these times if arriving by road.

Prices 1990 Season - for Clay Mine tour only:

Adults £1.50 Children/OAPs 75p
Family Ticket (2 adults & up to 4 children) £4.00
Discount prices for groups of 10 or more:
Adults £1.25 Children/OAPs 60p.

Groups should be pre-booked please to help us prevent hold-ups !

On most days you can make your day out even more enjoyable by travelling to Birkhill on a real steam train from Bo'ness Station.

Full details of train times from Bo'ness Heritage Trust or Bo'ness & Kinneil Railway. Telephone: Bo'ness [0506] 822298.

BO'NESS HERITAGE TRUST, 86a North Street, Bo'ness, West Lothian, EH51 9NF.
Telephone: Bo'ness [0506] 825855.

PATCHWAY

79. Patchway Station on the Bristol-South Wales line c 1905. The station originally named Patchway and Stoke Gifford, as the sign on the platform shows. The name was changed to Patchway only, in October 1908.

80. In October 1858 work began on the Bristol and South Wales Union Railway line form Bristol to New Passage. This involved building a 1,246 yard long tunnel with a steep gradient. Patchway new tunnel was built 22 years later when the line was doubled to cope with the increase in the traffic, when the Severn Tunnel was opened.

81. Stoke Gifford Church of St Michaels a 12th century church with a neat square tower, a steep path leading through the gateway to the church.

82. The interior of Stoke Gifford Church; with attractive oil lamps.

THE CHURCH AND VICARAGE, STOKE GIFFORD.   No. 363.

83. The Vicarage near the church, the postcard written from the vicarage in 1914. The house is built with a large garden surrounding it, including a greenhouse.

The Green, Stoke Gifford.   / No. 360

84. The Village Green at Stoke Gifford c1908, surrounded by the post office on the left and the village school on the right.

85. Stoke Gifford Green in the 1920s, not very different from the earlier picture No 82, the post office has been extended, and a War Memorial commemorating the local men killed in the 1914-18 War has been erected on the village green.

86. Stoke Gifford in the 1920s, children showing interest in the photographer, enjoying being part of the picture.